MOUNT RUSHMORE
Q & A
Answers to Frequently Asked Questions

by

Don "Nick" Clifford
Mount Rushmore Worker
1938-39-40

i

For information about ordering one or more copies of this book
contact the author at:

Rushmore Q & A
P.O. Box 263
Keystone, SD 57751

Website: www.mountrushmorecarver.com

© 2004 Carolyn M. Clifford
ISBN 0-9753006-0-1
Printed by Grelind Printing Center, Rapid City, SD USA
3rd Printing 2006

Contents

Preface

"Was it hard?" Believe it or not, this is the question asked most frequently of Nick Clifford, former Mount Rushmore driller and winchman. For several years, Nick has been answering questions asked by visitors at Mount Rushmore during the busiest tourist season. Now the questions and the answers, in Nick's own words, are compiled in this book as a way to offer you, the reader, a first hand account through the eyes and the recollections of one who was there.

When talking with Mount Rushmore visitors, Nick discovered that most are not particularly interested in the details; they are interested in his experiences and what it was like to work on a mountain carving. These are their questions, asked in their words.

The book is written in dialogue form and I have attempted to arrange the questions in sequence, although many questions and answers cannot be categorized. While reading Nick's answers, please remember that he is often speaking from first-hand experience. Other times he is telling about an experience of a fellow workman or expounding general information. Sometimes he injects his personal opinions. I have revised Nick's answers as little as possible in order to maintain their authenticity.

Nick is both humble and modest when talking about his work on Mount Rushmore. Most men did not have the opportunity to tell their stories publicly.

I have included a few humorous remarks and memorable conversations with visitors, just as I recorded them in my journal. I hope the reader enjoys the additions of these anecdotes, for it is the spontaneous reactions of the visitors that make Nick's days at Mount Rushmore so enjoyable.

Carolyn Clifford
"Nick's wife"

Acknowledgements

I want to express my gratitude to all the people who made this book possible, especially to my wonderful wife, Carolyn, who worked night and day these past months, taking my words, editing and revising where necessary. Through the years she kept a journal of the questions that visitors asked me at Mount Rushmore. Without her help this book would not be published. I thank her with much love!

Together, Carolyn and I are grateful to Aaron Moen for his advice and suggestions on getting started, to Diane Colvin for her helpful suggestions and editing, to Myron Shervheim for his title suggestions, and to Jim Popovich for verifying the factual accuracy of this material.

I am also grateful to Bruce Van Vort who first invited me to meet visitors, answer their questions and provided a place in the Mount Rushmore Gift Shop to do so.

Finally, I want to acknowledge hundreds of visitors to Mount Rushmore who unwittingly provided all the questions for this book. They showed me that most people ask similar questions about the mountain carving and that they are very interested in the answers.

Nick Clifford

Introduction

From the Mound to the Mountain

Donald Leo "Nick" Clifford, born in Pierre, SD on July 5, 1921, was the youngest of five children. His father, a cigar maker and a mining promoter, moved the family to Carter's Camp in the Black Hills. Shortly after moving to Keystone, SD in 1924, Nick's father left home. Nick would be 21 years old before he would see his father again.

With five young children and no job, Mrs. Clifford took in laundry to support the family. She washed three days a week and ironed four days a week. The children carried water in buckets from a local well and helped pump the hand-operated washing machine. The water and flat irons were heated on a wood stove. One of her customers was the Gutzon Borglum family.

At age seven Nick began delivering the *Rapid City Journal* in Keystone. He had more than 100 customers and became acquainted with everyone in town, including the men who worked on Mount Rushmore. To earn extra money, he chopped firewood for people on his paper route. He also rounded up a neighbor's cows and milked them for a quart of milk a day. Nick's mother was the janitor at the Keystone School where Nick and his brothers and sisters helped clean the building. They carried pails of drinking water and buckets of coal for the stoves in each classroom.

By age fourteen, Nick was managing one of the pool halls in Keystone. In the morning he opened the business, then cleaned, ran errands, sold candy and soft drinks, and racked the pool balls. At fifteen Nick quit

school to begin working at the Consolidated Feldspar
Company in both the mine and mill.

In spite of the
tough times Nick found
Keystone a good place
to grow up. There was
always something for
the kids to do after
chores. In the summer
they went swimming in
the creeks, exploring in
the hills, and "we
played baseball every
day, rain or shine," he
recalls. In the winter
there was ice skating
and sledding. A trip to
Rapid City for a movie

At 15, Nick began working at the Consolidated
Feldspar Company in Keystone, SD.

and shopping at the dime store was a big treat.

In 1938 Lincoln Borglum, an avid baseball fan, hired
Nick to work at Mount Rushmore primarily because he
was a good baseball player. Nick was playing baseball on
the Keystone team as well as the Junior Legion team in
Rapid City. Beginning with a variety of jobs below the
mountain, Nick later became a winchman on top of the
heads and a driller in front of the faces. For three years
Nick, a teenager, worked on the mountain carving that
has become one of the most famous sculptures in the
world.

CHAPTER 1

From Start to Finish

Q&A **Why was Mount Rushmore carved?**

Carving a mountain in the Black Hills was the idea of Doane Robinson, South Dakota State Historian. He read about the carving at Stone Mountain in Georgia, and he thought something similar to this would bring tourists to South Dakota. Eventually he contacted the sculptor, Gutzon Borglum, who received the support of U.S. Senator Peter Norbeck and Congressman William Williamson. The idea proved to be a good one because Mount Rushmore is the top visitor attraction in South Dakota.

Q&A **How was the site selected? Why did Mr. Borglum choose this location?**

In 1925, at the invitation of Doane Robinson, South Dakota State Historian, Mr. Borglum came to the Black Hills with his son, Lincoln, then thirteen years old. They spent about two weeks going through the Black Hills on horseback with a guide. Originally Mr. Robinson thought of carving western folk heroes in the Needles area near Harney Peak, but that was not suitable for a variety of reasons. Mr. Borglum said this project would be so monumental that it deserved national figures.

Mr. Borglum was looking for a fine-grain granite rock large enough for carving. He wanted it to face southeast so it would have the morning sunlight. Mount Rushmore had these characteristics, and when Mr. Borglum saw this granite rock he knew it was the right place. Only Mr. Borglum knew if the rock was suitable before the carving started, and he could not have been sure in the beginning.

How did Mr. Borglum know there was suitable rock?

I doubt if he knew that before starting the work. That is why Teddy Roosevelt is so far back. The carvers had to go back eighty-five feet from the original surface before good rock was found. There is only twenty-five feet of rock from the front of Roosevelt's face to the canyon in back of the heads.

With so many caves in the area, how did Mr. Borglum know he would not run into a cavity?

That was a chance Mr. Borglum took. Fortunately the granite was very solid and suitable for carving.

Why were these four presidents chosen?

George Washington was our first president and the Father of our country. Thomas Jefferson doubled the size of our country with the purchase of the Louisiana Territory in 1803. He also drafted the Declaration of Independence. Abraham Lincoln is credited with holding the nation together during the Civil War and he was called the Great Emancipator. Theodore Roosevelt supported the completion of the Panama Canal, which would have an effect on world trade. He also set aside some of the National Parks. Mr. Borglum, who was a friend of Teddy Roosevelt, chose the four presidents that he would carve.

How long did it take to carve Mount Rushmore?

It took fourteen years to carve the mountain, but the actual work time was less than seven years. Money was not available to work year around. Construction began on August 10, 1927, and the project was shut down on October 31, 1941.

Why is the carving not finished?

When comparing the carving to the model in the Sculptor's Studio, you can see there is still much work to be done. It was never finished for two reasons. First, Mr. Borglum passed away unexpectedly on March 6, 1941. Second, World War II was coming on and the United States Congress would no longer make appropriations for the mountain carving. Most of the spending would go towards the war effort.

Under Lincoln Borglum's supervision, the crew worked until the money ran out. On October 31, 1941, Lincoln closed down the project and called it finished. In my opinion, this was the right thing to do because it was Mr. Borglum's sculpture, and it should be left the way it was when he passed away.

Do you think it will be finished sometime?

No. The carving is a work of art as well as an engineering feat; therefore it would be inappropriate to resume work on Gutzon Borglum's sculpture.

Will there ever be another face added to Mount Rushmore?

There is not enough suitable rock for carving. Besides, it would cost too much and people could never agree on the "person" to put up there. I think it would cause a great controversy today.

Q. Were the four faces dedicated when done?

Washington was dedicated on July 4, 1930, with 2,500 people in attendance. Jefferson was dedicated on August 30, 1936, with 3,000 people in attendance. President Franklin D. Roosevelt came for that dedication. I was a Boy Scout in Keystone, and we all attended the dedication and shook hands with President Roosevelt. Of course, this was before I started working on Mount Rushmore.

Lincoln was dedicated on September 17, 1937, with 5,000 people in attendance. This was the 150th anniversary of the United States Constitution. Roosevelt was dedicated on July 2, 1939. The event also commemorated the 50th anniversary of South Dakota statehood. Twelve thousand people attended and watched the first fireworks display at Mount Rushmore.

On July 3, 1991, President George Bush dedicated Mount Rushmore during the Golden Anniversary Celebration. Because of security related to the President's visit, the crowd was limited to 3,500 people. Twenty-two former Rushmore workers attended the celebration. The national media covered the event, which gave Mount Rushmore tremendous publicity.

Q. How often do you have fireworks here?

The second fireworks display at Mount Rushmore was 59 years later on July 5, 1998, as part of the Independence Day celebration. It was also my seventy-seventh birthday. I was called on stage in the amphitheater and introduced to the large crowd that stood and sang *Happy Birthday* to me. It was a very memorable moment for me. Fireworks on July 3rd have become an annual event at Mount Rushmore, drawing crowds of several thousand people to the memorial and thousands more watching from a distance.

How did Mount Rushmore get its name?

Charles Rushmore, a young attorney from New York City, came to Keystone in 1885 representing clients who had mining claims in the Black Hills. Local men guided him through the Black Hills on horseback looking at the mines. When Mr. Rushmore saw this particular granite rock he asked about its name. To make an impression on him, the men said it did not have a name, so we will call it Mount Rushmore.

Four decades later when Gutzon Borglum began carving Mount Rushmore, Charles Rushmore donated $5000 to the project. The mountain had several different names until July 1930, when the Board of Geographic Names officially recognized the name *Mount Rushmore.*

" After traveling in the western United States and the Canadian Rockies, a couple from Virginia said they took extra time to come to Mount Rushmore. They attended the Evening Lighting Ceremony.

The next day they told Nick, "We have been naming the highlights of our trip. After seeing all that beauty, we decided this is the highlight so far." "

Nick Clifford, sitting on a winch he operated on Washington's head sixty-three years earlier, explains one of the "close-calls" during construction.

Construction

How was Mount Rushmore carved?

The first thing Mr. Borglum did was make a model of the four faces. Then workmen took measurements on the model. A small arm that extended over the heads on the model could be rotated like a protractor. A plumb bob was attached to the arm, and lowered to the point of measurement. The same thing was used on top of the mountain, only it was a much larger device. It was called a pointing machine, which is why the men who did that work were called pointers. By setting the degree and dropping the plumb bob, they transferred the measurement from the model to the mountain. An inch on the model was equivalent to a foot on the mountain. The pointers had a very precise job because a wrong measurement on the model could mean disaster on the mountain carving.

What is the model made from?

The model in the Sculptor's Studio is made from plaster of paris over a wooden frame. Mr. Borglum changed the model nine times over the course of fourteen years.

Which president was carved first? Were they carved in order? What was the point of reference? Was one face finished before the next one started?

Washington was the first face to be started, Jefferson next, then Lincoln, and finally Roosevelt. The nose was always the point of reference and carved first because it protrudes the farthest. The carvers did not finish one face completely before starting the next one.

Mr. Borglum viewed the sculpture from a distance as he rode up in the bucket. He fine-tuned the faces many times to make changes as he saw necessary. Work was being done on each face until closing in October of 1941.

Is there a danger of a nose falling off?

No, barring an earthquake or some other natural disaster. At least I hope not.

Where did the power come from?

There were no roads or power lines to the mountain in 1927. Rushmore needed electricity, so the struggle began to get both. The first power came from a donated, used submarine diesel engine. Located in Keystone, the engine ran the generator, and power poles and lines were built to the mountain. This turned out to be unsatisfactory due to many breakdowns and the engine finally blew up.

The Holy Terror Mine in Keystone started another power company, which furnished the power to Mount Rushmore as well as to Keystone. The power came on at 7 a.m. and at 10:55 p.m. the lights in Keystone would blink to let Keystone residents know the lights were going off. Keystone did not have power from 11 p.m. to 7 a.m.

Q A How did you get the power to the top of the mountain? How many air compressors did you have?

The air compressors were located at the base of the mountain near the blacksmith shop and hoist house. The air was piped to the top of the mountain in a six-inch steel pipe and many hoses connected the pipe to the air hammers used by the drillers.

In the beginning two compressors were used. Mr. Borglum wanted another compressor, but for lack of electric power it was not possible. When he got more electric power at the mountain, he used a third compressor that allowed more air, and he could use more drillers on top.

Q A What was in the buildings on top of the mountain? How long did it take to build them?

The two winch houses were built to surround several hand cranked winches on Washington and Jefferson. An A-frame was on top of Roosevelt's head, which is where the tramway came to the top of the mountain. The building on top of Lincoln's head was a maintenance shop where the workmen also used to eat lunch and get out of the weather. Small models of the presidents, tools and supplies were kept in the buildings on top. There were many stairways and ladders and a few smaller buildings – one was an "outhouse." I am sure Mr. Borglum started out with bare necessities and added the buildings as needed.

Buildings on top of heads during construction. (From left) Maintenance building, A-frame for tramway, and two winch houses. Nick worked in the winch house on Washington's head (far right).

How did the cable for the cable car get put up there?

One of the first things the workmen did in 1927 was build a tramway to the top of the mountain. This was the best and fastest means to get materials and equipment to the top. The workmen anchored one of the hand cranked winches in the rock where they wanted the cable, hooked on to the cable down below the mountain with a smaller cable, and cranked it up by hand. Then they anchored it in the rock on top of the mountain.

The first car was a round steel barrel similar to what was used in the mines for hoisting ore out of the mine. This barrel was used for a number of years and no one except Mr. Borglum and Lincoln could ride in it. It served a good purpose until the wooden cage was built.

How did the workers get up on top? How long did it take?

When carving began a wooden stairway was built all the way to the top and the men would walk both ways. It took about fifteen minutes to walk up the stairs. The record was four and one-half minutes. In 1936 a wooden cage was built and five men would ride up together, but everyone walked back down. The term *cable car* is used today, but the workmen called it either the bucket or the cage.

When I started work in 1938, I rode up in the bucket and walked down the stairway. It took about seven minutes for the bucket to go up, but it came down a lot faster. We did not get paid for the time going up and down.

What was the biggest mistake?

Originally Jefferson was to be on Washington's left side, and only three faces were to be carved – Washington, Jefferson, and Lincoln. When they found the rock on the left was not suitable for carving, the partially completed face was blasted away, and the head of Jefferson was started again on the right side of Washington. Many hours of work and many valuable dollars were lost.

I do not think it was really a mistake because no one knew what the granite was like until the drillers began removing rock. There are many different stories about this, but I settle for bad granite. It worked out for the best because I think the monument looks better with the four faces as they are today.

How did you "erase" Jefferson on Washington's left side?

The men drilled deep holes in the granite, loaded them with dynamite and just blasted it off. This took place in 1934, long before I was working on the carving.

Are there any patches on the faces? What was the patch made from?

There is only one patch which is on Jefferson's lip. The drillers hit a section of quartz rock that could not be carved, so they cut it out and made a granite plug, so to speak, which was anchored in that area. If the viewers do not know what it is, the patch cannot be seen.

What are the streaks on Jefferson's face?

The dark lines are visible on Jefferson's right eye and cheek, converging at the lip. These lines are cracks in the granite, which were discovered when rough rock was being removed. Under Mr. Borglum's direction the position of Jefferson's head was tilted back, and as a result, the cracks run through Jefferson's cheek instead of through his nose. The cracks are watched very carefully.

How big are the faces?

The heads are approximately sixty feet high with noses twenty feet long. The mouths are eighteen feet wide. The eyes are approximately eleven feet wide and five feet high. If these features had a body, it would be the equivalent of a man standing 465 feet tall!

Mr. Borglum left a shaft of granite in each eye representing the pupil. This artistic technique along with the natural light and shadow created a life-like expression in the eyes of each president.

What is the elevation of Mount Rushmore?

On top of Washington's head the elevation is 5,725 feet. The Visitor Center is 5,245 feet.

Why did you leave the two rocks on Lincoln's head?

Originally there were three large round rocks on top of and to the right of Lincoln's head. The workers nicknamed the rocks the "three monkeys." The rock on the left needed to be removed so it was drilled, loaded with dynamite, and

Mount Rushmore, as it appeared before carving began in 1927. The "three monkeys" are balancing on the edge of the rock.

blasted. To the surprise of everyone, the rock came off in one large chunk. The workmen who watched the blast thought the boulder was going to wipe out the blacksmith shop and the compressor house; fortunately, it stopped in the rock pile below the faces.

Q & A — Did it take four hundred men to do the job?

The Workers Recognition Plaque has 395 names taken from the payroll records of the National Park Service. Some may have worked only a day, a week or a month, and never came back. Quite a few men worked the full fourteen years; many worked eight to ten years.

Most people do not realize that Mr. Borglum trained between thirty-five and forty men who lived in Keystone. When construction at the mountain would shut down, they had to find other jobs. These men were family men who needed a job to support their families.

All of these men were dedicated to Mr. Borglum and his task, so when money was available to begin work again, they went back to their jobs at Mount Rushmore. Mr. Borglum did not have to train a new crew every year. Without these dedicated and experienced men there would not be a mountain carving, as we know it today.

How much did it cost to carve Mount Rushmore?

It cost $989,992.32 which was twice as much as Mr. Borglum expected. Most of the money came from the U.S. government. I think it was a good investment, not only for the federal government but also for the State of South Dakota.

Funding for the mountain sculpture was Mr. Borglum's biggest problem. In the beginning Mr. Borglum expected the money to come from private donations and corporations. Schools around the country had fund-raisers in the 1930s, and youngsters saved nickels and dimes for the carving.

Were tourists ever allowed on top of the heads?

Yes, during construction tourists were allowed on top of the mountain. A guide would take them up on the stairway. He charged twenty-five cents per person and made more money than the men working on the faces! Walkways and stairways connected the buildings on top of the heads and visitors could walk around up there, but never where men were working.

Mr. Borglum's original plans included a stairway to the top for the public to use when the monument was completed. Those plans went by the wayside and today the public is not allowed on top of the mountain.

Q. Is there a lot of maintenance to do on the faces? How are the cracks filled?

A. The National Park Service is responsible for the maintenance on the faces. Every fall a maintenance man checks all the cracks and looks for new ones. Computers monitor the cracks continually to check for movement and changes.

During construction the cracks were filled with a mixture of white lead, linseed oil and granite dust from the drilling. All that material has been removed and the cracks refilled with silicone caulk that allows for expansion and contraction, which was not possible with the old method.

" At the lighting ceremony on July 2, 2000, a lady who was visiting with Nick asked him his age. Nick answered, "I will be 79 in three days."

"I am a dermatologist," she said, "and you don't have any wrinkles; your skin looks wonderful."

Always ready with a witty answer, Nick said, "It's dark enough so you can't see them." "

CHAPTER 3
Blasting, Honeycombing and Bumping

Q&A Was the dynamite a fire fuse or electric? Did everyone have to leave the mountain when blasting?

The caps were electric, and in the beginning they were set off by a plunger. In later years when the powder men were shooting more holes, electricity was used to set them off because the plunger did not generate enough current. The workers did not leave the mountain, but the powder men made sure everyone was on top of the heads away from all the flying rock. The powder men blasted at 12 noon during the lunch break and again at 4 p.m.

Q&A Why was the dynamite cut into small pieces?

When the drillers and powder men were taking off the outer layer of granite, deep holes were drilled and full sticks of dynamite were used. When getting closer to what would be the finished faces, shallow holes were drilled and the powder men used short pieces of dynamite, 1.5 to 2 inches long. They were powerful enough to blow off the rock and not harm the granite behind the drill holes.

When they blasted, how did they know how much to take off, like if they were doing the lips?

Dynamite was never used to carve the fine features. Dynamite was used to remove about ninety percent of the outer layer of granite – the rough, surface rock. No blasting was done when they got near the finished surface; then it was all handwork.

How many misfires?

I do not recall any misfires with the blasting. The powder men were good and knew their job. An incident I do remember was the day that lightning set off a charge. There was only one man drilling on Washington's lapel when a lightning storm came up about three miles from the mountain. The powder men had the holes loaded with dynamite, ready for blasting. Because electric caps were used, when the lightning hit at the mountain, it unexpectedly set off the dynamite while the workman was still in front of the face. It blew him into the air away from the rock and blew his shoes off. Coming down, he hit hard against the rock. It shook him up real good, but he was a tough guy and came back to work the next day. He never found his shoes. From that time on the powder men were careful never to load holes where men were working.

What is the rock with all the holes? Were the holes for dynamite?

The next to the last step of carving the faces was called honeycombing simply because the procedure resembled a honeycomb. Holes were drilled in rows about one inch apart to weaken the

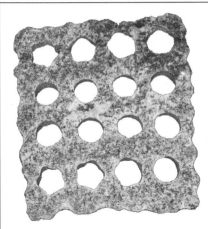

Honeycomb rock that has both round and star-shaped holes.

granite so the rock could be knocked off with a sharp pointed chisel and hammer. Dynamite was never put in the honeycomb holes. Sometimes a large piece of honeycomb would be taken off, but in order to do it the carver had to hit in each hole with his chisel all around the rock before it would break off. This was not done often because it took too much time. All of us could have carried a honeycomb rock home every day, but we were anxious to get home, and to us it was just a piece of rock.

Why are the holes in the honeycomb rock different shapes?

One of the honeycomb rocks that I have as a souvenir has sixteen holes, and it is unique because the holes are both star-shaped and round. The drill steel in the jackhammer was supposed to spin. If there was a problem with the jackhammer, it was hitting in and out instead of spinning, causing the holes to be star shaped exactly like the end of the drill steel.

> " One little boy insisted on holding the heavy honeycomb rock while having his picture taken, so Nick helped him hold the rock. After the picture was snapped he told Nick, "You hurt my finger." "

Q & A: Did anyone sell the honeycomb rock?

Some of the rocks were sold. The carvers would send a few down to the hoist house; tourists would notice the rocks with drill holes and ask the hoist operator if they were for sale. He told them some kind of story, and sometimes the tourists would make a deal for a few dollars. When Mr. Borglum found out about it, that was the end of it. Nowadays some honeycomb rocks are worth hundreds of dollars, depending on the number of holes, and very few are still around.

> " Nick was telling four bikers from Pennsylvania about the honeycomb rocks being scarce and valuable today. He said, "If I knew then what I know now, I would have carried one home every day."
> Quickly changing the subject, one of the men replied, "If I knew then what I know now, I would be living in a one room house and single." "

Q & A: How did the faces get so smooth and white?

The rocks nearby the sculpture are a dark colored granite, the same as the mountain in the beginning. After the outer layer of granite was blasted off and the honeycombing process finished, the surface still had rough edges of granite. The last step of finishing the faces was called bumping. The tool used was an air driven hammer about twelve inches long with a four-pronged piece of steel that both spun around and hit in and out against the granite. It moved very fast and knocked off the rough edges, smoothing the faces and giving them a white color. They are as smooth as a concrete driveway. Nothing is ever done to clean the faces, and I, personally, hope they stay this way forever.

CHAPTER 4
Nick's Jobs on Mount Rushmore

How did you get the job on Mount Rushmore?

I was six years old and living in Keystone when Mr. Borglum started to carve the mountain in 1927, so I grew up with the carving. Many of the men who worked at Rushmore were on my paper route. I knew some of the men from my job in the pool hall in Keystone.

I went to the top of the mountain many times before getting a job. The mail truck came to Keystone every weekday, and often I put my bicycle in the back of the truck and rode up to the mountain with the driver. The cable car hoist operator, Ed Hayes, would telephone up to Lincoln Borglum saying, "Nick is down here and wants to ride up." Lincoln always answered, "Okay, send him up." I rode up with the next load of supplies, spent a few hours on top visiting with the

Nick Clifford, left, and Philip Watson were "little rabbits" in a school program in 1927, the year Gutzon Borglum began carving Mount Rushmore.

workmen, then ran down the stairway, and coasted back to Keystone on my bicycle. I was looking for a job, of course, but they did not hire anyone my age.

Lincoln Borglum was a great baseball fan, and in 1938 he decided that Mount Rushmore should sponsor the Keystone baseball team. Lincoln hired me because I was a pretty good baseball player, but I like to think he also knew I worked hard. We went to the State Tournament in Aberdeen, SD the first year and also in 1939, which was the year we had a very good team.

Q/A What was your job?

I had many jobs. My first job was cutting firewood, which was used to heat the café, the bunkhouse, and other buildings. The café was open to the public and the bunkhouse was where some of the single men lived. Next I worked with a stone mason, mixing mud to build slate rock walls. Mr. Borglum liked slate walls, and some are still standing. We quarried the slate from the rocks below and to the right of the faces, and hauled it with a stone boat pulled by a team of horses.

Clifford family photo (ca. 1932)

Nick with his new bicycle in front of his home in Keystone.

Mr. Borglum wanted a new studio. My brother, Charles, and I helped build the existing sculptor's studio. Charles cut the logs nearby and they were skidded in with a team of horses. The winter of 1938 I peeled each log with a drawknife.

22

The logs dried that winter and in the spring of 1939 we started putting up the building. When it was finished, five of us men moved Mr. Borglum's model into the new studio. Later, a fireplace was built in the new studio and I cut a piece of granite below Roosevelt's chin in the shape of an arrowhead that was used for the keystone rock.

Nick, donning his new baseball uniform.

Eventually I went to work in the winchhouse on top of Washington where we hand-cranked, up or down, the men who were working in the bosun chairs. Ed Young, who had been a winchman for several years, trained me in the winchhouse. From there I graduated to the job of driller. First I drilled to the right of Lincoln's beard, but most of my drilling was below the chin of Roosevelt.

How did you move the models?

In order to be moved the model was sawed into four sections, placed on planks with pipe rollers, and moved down the steps from Mr. Borglum's original studio to the new (existing) studio. Then the four sections were put back together again. They needed quite a bit of patching. Mr. Borglum was gone at the time, so Jim LaRue and I thought we could patch them. We went to Gothman's shingle mill to get long wood shavings, then mixed the shavings with plaster of paris in a wash tub, and patched all the cracks and holes. They looked as good as new to us! When Mr. Borglum returned he was upset and wanted to know who did this job. I do not think he ever found out. The model was no longer to scale, and he sent to New York for another sculptor to come and redo our job.

 Did you take an apprenticeship to work here?

Model of George Washington, prepared for the move to Borglum's new studio. Left to right: Charles Clifford, Gale Wilcox, Ray Daley, Bob McNally, and Nick Clifford.

No. I knew how to run a jackhammer and that was the main requirement. When I started drilling Lincoln Borglum told me where to drill and how to do it. I learned to run a jackhammer in the mines before coming to work at Mount Rushmore.

Did it take more than one man in the winch house to move a man?

Generally one man could move a man in a harness. When we were moving one of the wooden boxes it took two men. If Mr. Borglum was in the harness we were extra careful.

We had two winch houses, one was on Washington's head, where I worked, and the other was on Jefferson's head. Two men worked in each winch house taking care of ten or twelve winches. Being a winchman was a good job because we were out of the weather and we could sit down when no orders came for moving the drillers.

How did the drillers use the channel iron?

The channel iron was a piece of steel of different lengths with teeth at the end. It worked from a jackhammer. Instead of spinning around, it hit up and down. We drilled holes as close to each other as possible, then we would insert the channel iron in the jackhammer and cut between each hole. We would drill two or three holes underneath the piece of rock, depending on how much rock we were going to remove. Next we would use feathers and wedges, which were pieces of steel, and with a sledgehammer, drive the wedge between the feathers. Eventually the rock would break off. Many of these rocks can be seen today from the Presidential Trail.

How did you keep from dropping tools when you needed to stop for something?

A good number of drill steel were dropped. If you could sort through the muck pile below the faces, I am sure you would find many souvenirs. That area is off limits to the public now.

Why were the jackhammers on chains?

Sometimes a driller would put a piece of

Using planks and pipe rollers, Nick, left, and the other workmen moved the model down the steps to Borglum's new studio.

drill steel in a drill hole above where he was working, then attach a chain to it. When he was drilling straight in, it took the weight off the jackhammer, and he only had to push in on the jackhammer. It made drilling much easier.

How much did you make? Who paid you and how often were you paid?

When I first started I was paid fifty cents an hour doing the various jobs down below the mountain. When I went on top as a winchman I made fifty-five cents an hour. When I started drilling I made sixty-five cents an hour. We worked eight hours a day, six days a week. Some men made 75 cents an hour and others made $1.00 an hour. The carvers made as much as $1.25 an hour, which was a good wage in the 1930s.

Mostly the United States government financed this project. We were paid twice a month and received a government check. We received no overtime, and retirement plans were unheard of in those days.

Clifford Family Photo (2000)

Gutzon Borglum's Studio, built in 1939, is known today as the Sculptor's Studio.

What is the difference between a carver and a driller?

Mr. Borglum had eight or ten men who worked on the mountain carving from the beginning and he trained these men as carvers. They did most all of the finish work - the eyes, nose, chin, etc. – wherever it was delicate and precise work. The rest of us just drilled a lot of holes; we were drillers. In general I suppose all of us were carvers, but I like to make a distinction between the two in respect to the trained men who did the finish work.

How did your brother get the job on Mount Rushmore?

My mother did the laundry for the Denison family. John Denison was the superintendent at the mountain at the time. I guess he knew we needed extra money, so he gave my oldest brother, Charles, a job. My uncle, Albert "Babe" Stangle, also worked on the carving in the early 1930s.

"Did you sing while you were working?" asked a lady from Chicago.

"Have you ever heard a jackhammer?" Nick asked.

"No," she replied.

"One jackhammer makes a lot of noise, so there was no point in singing. Besides, I'm not much of a singer anyway."

Orville Worman, drilling on the head of Roosevelt.

CHAPTER 5
Other Jobs on Mount Rushmore

Q **What did the blacksmith do?**

A The blacksmith made many of the tools we used and he sharpened all of the drill steel. When all of the men were drilling, we went through about four hundred drill steel a day. The blacksmith always had a helper. The last blacksmith had graduated from helper to blacksmith, and he was a very good one, I might add.

Q **How long did a sharpened drill bit last?**

A There was no set time for how long a sharp piece of steel would last. We could drill one to two feet before a tool needed to be sharpened. It all depended on how good a temper the blacksmith got on the steel. There was no use trying to drill with a dull piece of steel because you were just wasting time. Nowadays we have carbide bits that last much longer and require a different method of sharpening.

Q **How did the supplies get on top of the mountain?**

A All the drill steel went up on the tramway. We had one man on top who would meet the bucket, unload the sharpened steel or other supplies, then load it back up with the dull steel and whatever else needed to be sent down. By way of a harness, a ladder or scaffolding, this man also took the sharpened steel to the drillers working on the faces, picking up their dull steel bits that needed to be sharpened. Down below, the man working in the hoist house delivered the dull steel to the blacksmith shop.

What did the compressor operator do?

He did not have a very physical job, but it was an important one. When I worked on Mount Rushmore there were three air compressors driven by electric motors that furnished all the compressed air for the jackhammers on top of the mountain. The compressor operator made sure the compressors were working at top performance. He also blew the air whistle for starting and stopping work at 7:30 a.m. and 4 p.m., as well as at 12 noon and 12:30 p.m. for our lunch break. He seemed to have a very accurate watch. There were no coffee breaks in those days!

> " A family from Texas could not find a motel room closer than Mitchell, SD. They told Nick, "We drove five hundred miles out of our way to see Mount Rushmore. Meeting you here made it all worthwhile." "

What did the call boy do?

The call boy sat on the rock on Lincoln's head where he could see all the men working. He knew which men were assigned to each winch house. The men motioned to him when they wanted to be raised or lowered. Then he would let the men in the winch houses know, in earlier years by "calling," and in later years by microphone. We had speakers in the winch houses. In cold weather the call boy sat in a small shack.

How many men were working at one time?

At any one time, the best I can remember, there were thirty five or forty men, counting the workers both down below and on top of the mountain. There were a few jobs for women as well. Some worked in the café. The caretaker's mother explained the construction project to visitors in Mr. Borglum's first studio. Other women sold a few postcards and souvenirs. Mr. Borglum always had a secretary.

Did you work in the winter?

Ordinarily we worked from April to November, depending on the weather and available funds. I think the winter of 1938 was the only winter of continuous work. Because of the cold and snow, it did not pan out very well. Canvas was put over the scaffolding with fifty-five gallon barrels used to burn wood or coke (a by-product of coal that burns with intense heat and little smoke) to keep warm. Not much was accomplished and some days the men on top could not work at all, so they never tried it again. Most of the time there was not enough money to work year around.

Where did the men who worked on Mt. Rushmore live?

Most of the men lived in Keystone or nearby. Some of the single men lived in the boarding house at the mountain. The caretaker and his wife lived in a family dwelling at the mountain. All these buildings are gone now, unfortunately, for they would have significant historical value today.

Do the workers have a reunion?

We had our first reunion at the State Game Lodge in 1952, which was twenty-five years after the carving started. Some of the men and women who lived out of state used to come back over the Fourth of July. In 1991 when President Bush came for the 50th Anniversary of the completion of the sculpture, about twenty-two former workers were in attendance. Most of those workers have passed away now.

> " A mother told her children, "This is a historical man." "You have that right," Nick said, "At my age I am a historical man." "

Clifford family photo (1991)

Mount Rushmore Workers. Seated: Matt Reilly, Edwald Hayes, Chuck Hallsted; Middle: Orville Worman, Don "Nick" Clifford, Ray Berg, Melba Payne, Bill Tallman; Back: Chuck Sheely, Don Morrison

CHAPTER 6

Safety and Accidents

What kinds of safety measures were used?

Safety was the number one priority with both Mr. Borglum and Lincoln Borglum. Lincoln and the foremen were very careful where they placed the men to drill. Men would not be positioned above each other in case something dropped. We had respirators, which were not very efficient, and most men did not wear them. One of my friends cut a hole in his mask so he could smoke his pipe and when he saw Mr. Borglum coming he put it away. Mr. Borglum was quite upset about that. We did not have hard hats, earplugs, or steel-toed boots. Most of the safety equipment used nowadays was unheard of back then. This was long before the safety measures required by OSHA.

What was the worst accident?

The worst accident was on the tramway when five men were in the bucket. When the bucket got near the top a pin sheared off at the hoist house, which let the bucket free wheel back down. The tramway was equipped with a homemade emergency brake consisting of a piece of pipe with a long chain on it. When you pulled the pipe down it pressed against the main one-inch cable, slowing down the bucket. When the accident happened, one man used the emergency brake to slow down the bucket. Another man in the bucket kind of panicked. He grabbed the chain and pulled too hard on the brake, which broke it. The bucket came in for landing between the blacksmith shop and the compressor house.

I suppose we all wondered, at one time or another, what we would do if something happened. In this case, one of the five men, Hap Anderson, thought if he jumped out going by the blacksmith shop he would land on the roof and not get hurt, but he could not judge his speed and he slammed into the rocks below. He was in the hospital about three months, but he came back to work eventually. Had he stayed in the bucket, he probably would not have been hurt too badly. The four men who stayed in the bucket were not hurt, but they were really shook up.

Where were you when the accident happened?

I was standing on the platform waiting to go up with the next load. The injured workmen were taken to the hospital in Rapid City by car since we did not have ambulance service out of town in those days.

Did you hang in one of those bosun chairs? I'm surprised no one fell out.

I did some work in the bosun chair and found it very hard. A driller had to hold the jackhammer, which weighs 40 to 50 pounds, plus some tools. It was difficult to apply the necessary pressure working in a bosun chair.

During construction the workers did not use the term *bosun chair*. All of us called the chair a *harness*. Workers used them when they were lowered over the mountain to drill or perform other jobs. Once a man was strapped

Gutzon Borglum (right) in the wooden cage and Lincoln Borglum on the loading platform at the top of Roosevelt's head. Notice the chain hooked to the pipe that was the safety brake.

in, he could not fall out.

Q&A Did anyone die during the construction?

No. There were many bumps and bruises and some close calls, but the project had no fatalities during the fourteen years of construction. Mr. Borglum was very safety conscious, especially for that time. He knew this was a very dangerous task.

" A mother told her young son, "This man helped carve Mount Rushmore."

The boy gazed at Nick for a few moments and said, "Anybody who carved Mount Rushmore should be dead by now!" "

" With tearful eyes a woman in a tour group told Nick, "Seeing Mount Rushmore in pictures just does not compare to seeing it in person." She shook his hand twice and thanked him repeatedly "for what you did for me."

Another woman in the group joined her and began listening to the conversation. Finally she asked her friend, "What did he do for you? I saw you five minutes ago and you were just fine."

"This man worked on Mount Rushmore," the lady said. Then they both were awestruck! "

CHAPTER 7

Gutzon Borglum, Sculptor

What was Mr. Borglum like? Was he a hard taskmaster?

I remember him as a generous and good man. The workmen called him either Mr. Borglum or The Chief. There are a lot of stories, both good and bad, about him; however, every famous person is both admired and criticized. He was sixty years old when he began carving Mount Rushmore, and he dedicated the last fourteen years of his life to the carving. Both Mr. Borglum and Senator Peter Norbeck deserve a lot of credit from the State of South Dakota.

Certainly Mr. Borglum was a hard taskmaster because he knew what needed to be done, and he wanted the work done his way. There was no allowance for mistakes; if too much rock was removed, obviously, it could not be replaced.

Was Mr. Borglum at Mount Rushmore all the time?

When Mr. Borglum arrived he brought along Jesse Tucker, an experienced helper on Stone Mountain, Georgia, and put him in charge of setting up all the facilities at Mount Rushmore. Mr. Borglum was there a lot of the time, but he always had a foreman who was in charge in his absence. Towards the end of the project Lincoln Borglum was the Superintendent. Mr. Borglum, who was responsible for all the promotion for Mount Rushmore, also spent a lot of time in Washington, D.C., convincing Congress to appropriate more money.

Where did Mr. Borglum live?

In the beginning he lived in Keystone with his family. Eventually he bought a ranch west of Hermosa, SD and he commuted to the mountain every day. I never knew Mr. Borglum to drive a car – he always had a driver.

How did Gutzon Borglum die and where is he buried?

On their way to Washington, Mr. Borglum and his wife, Mary, stopped in Chicago for a speaking engagement. While there he saw a doctor who recommended minor surgery. He died unexpectedly about two weeks later on March 6, 1941. The Rushmore workers were among those who attended a memorial service at the Keystone Congregational Church the following Sunday after receiving news of his death.

Gutzon Borglum is buried at Forest Lawn Cemetery in Glendale, California. Congress approved his burial at Mount Rushmore, but the family decided on California.

> "Many parents tell Nick that they came to Mount Rushmore with their parents when they were young, and now they are bringing their own children to see it. Nick will often tell those children that when they grow up and get married, they will have to bring their children to Mount Rushmore too. One little boy said quickly, "I'm never going to get married and have kids.""

Where is Lincoln Borglum buried?

Lincoln Borglum died on January 27, 1986. Lincoln and Mary Anne Borglum are buried in the City Cemetery, a huge old cemetery in the heart of San Antonio, Texas. Their headstone is a large piece of Rushmore granite with a white marble plaque inscribed with the names and dates. It took an act of Congress for permission to remove the five hundred-pound granite rock from Mount Rushmore.

Rushmore granite headstone on graves of Lincoln and Mary Anne Borglum.

MCMXCVIII

Nick and Carolyn Clifford behind granite capstone in the Hall of Records.

40

CHAPTER 8

Hall of Records

Q.A. What was Borglum's plan for the Hall of Records?

There is a small canyon behind the faces. The tunnel for the Hall of Records is carved into the rock beyond the canyon, not into the rock where the faces are carved. Work began in 1938 and the tunnel was drilled approximately seventy or eighty feet. Mr. Borglum made plans for a grand museum with glass entrance doors, large rooms containing statues and texts of the historical documents of the United States. He wanted to build a stairway to the museum so visitors could walk up to it.

Mr. Borglum always said there was no record of why the Egyptian pyramids and the Sphinx were carved, and he wanted a permanent record for future generations to know the meaning of the United States and Mount Rushmore. The work halted the following year when Congress and other supporters encouraged him to complete the presidents first. Mr. Borglum's plans went by the wayside and the Hall of Records was never completed according to his original plans.

Q.A. Did you ever work in the Hall of Records?

No. The dust was very bad in there, especially when drilling deeper into the tunnel. There was no water on top of Mount Rushmore, so all the drilling was dry which caused so much dust.

Miners used water in the drilling equipment to cut down on the dust when drilling in a tunnel or enclosed space.

Q&A How was the Hall of Records completed?

Over the years the Borglum family was determined to complete the Hall of Records in some form. Nowadays, of course, it would cost millions of dollars to complete it according to the original plans. Finally the Borglum family received the support of Mount Rushmore Superintendent Dan Wenk, and a Hall of Records Committee was formed that made plans for finishing the hall on a smaller scale without federal funding. Drilling began on a vault just 26 by 16 inches and 4 feet deep in June of 1998. The vault, lined with titanium, is located in the entrance of the tunnel.

Seven weeks later on August 9th my wife and I joined a group of 119 people who hiked up the rocky, dirt trail for the ceremony that completed the Hall of Records. A box made from teakwood, highly resistant to rotting, first was lowered into the chamber. Then sixteen porcelain enamel panels were lowered, one by one, into the teakwood box. Etched onto the panels were the following records:

> Text of the United States Constitution
> The Bill of Rights
> Text of the Declaration of Independence
> Text of the Gettysburg Address

Information about Mount Rushmore National Memorial, the four Presidents, Gutzon Borglum, and how and why the monument was carved was included on the porcelain panels.

Finally, a twelve hundred pound piece of granite was

placed on top of the vault, sealing the documents for perhaps thousands of years. Inscribed on the beautiful black capstone are words spoken by Sculptor Gutzon Borglum in 1930 at the dedication of Washington.

"…let us place there, carved high, as close to heaven as we can, the words of our leaders, their faces, to show posterity what manner of men they were. Then breathe a prayer that these records will endure until the wind and rain alone shall wear them away."

Q & A How did the granite capstone get up there?

The capstone was airlifted into the canyon by helicopter. It was designed so several men lifted it with steel pipes and carefully placed it on the vault. Now it is a time capsule, which may be opened some day.

After conversing with Nick about Mount Rushmore, a man told his wife, "This man was on the TV program that made you cry."

Keystone Team, 1938. Front row: Howdy Peterson, Nick Clifford, Glen Jones, and Ted Crawford; Back row: Casey Jones, Merle Peterson, Lincoln Borglum, Gutzon Borglum, Red Anderson, unknown, Frank Hughes, and Al Johnson. The little boy in front is Frank's son.

CHAPTER 9

Baseball Team

Q **What does baseball have to do with Mount Rushmore?**

A Lincoln Borglum was a great baseball fan and he wanted Mount Rushmore to sponsor the baseball team in Keystone. So in 1938 and 1939 he hired men who were good baseball players and that is how I got the job. We practiced after work and played games on Sunday afternoon. Consisting mostly of Rushmore workers, the first year we were called the Keystone team. Red Anderson, one of the carvers, was the manager.

The first year we did not have uniforms, but that did not keep us from having a good team. On July 18, 1938, a headline on the sports page of the *Rapid City Journal* stated **Keystone About Faces To Stop Dohertys, 6-1.** The article begins, *"Keystone, previously considered harmless and a permanent occupant of the cellar position in the city league, grew fangs overnight and turned out to be the Big Bad Wolf in disguise Sunday as the Dohertys, unsuspectingly walked into an ambush, to find bats swinging about their ears and balls bouncing past them, as Keystone brought over six runs and chalked up a 6 to 1 victory."* From then on, we were on our way...

Q **Who attended the baseball games?**

A The people living in Keystone supported the team and attended the games. We went on to win the regional tournament in Rapid City, which qualified us for the State Amateur Baseball Tournament in Aberdeen. We lost the first game in Aberdeen, but just getting to the state level was a great way to end our first season. The players and the fans were very proud of our team!

What position did you play?

I was a pitcher and a right outfielder. In those days a pitcher usually pitched the whole game. When another man was pitching, I was playing in right field.

What kind of pitches did you throw?

Back in those days, we had no one to train us, so about all we did was throw a curve or two. I mostly relied on throwing as hard as I could and it worked out pretty well.

What teams did you play?

Nearly every small town had a baseball team at that time, and Rapid City usually had a couple of teams. The fans attended the games we played in other towns too. Baseball was a popular sport and supported by every community that had a team in the 1930s and 1940s.

Did you go to the state tournament in 1939?

We really had a good team in 1939. We went to the State Amateur Baseball Tournament again and ended in third place. Mr. Borglum came to Aberdeen for some of the games, which pleased all the spectators and fans. He was well known for his mountain carving by that time. I remember when he stopped the game and walked out on the field to say something to third baseman, Howdy Peterson. Howdy never remembered what he said, but it had nothing to do with baseball. Mr. Borglum enjoyed the attention.

This was an exciting time for everyone. Playing baseball added some camaraderie between the players who worked together on the mountain. Lincoln Borglum ordered uniforms and jackets for us that year. The uniforms were cream colored and had Rushmore Memorial in red letters on the front. Our jackets were red with an emblem of Mount Rushmore on the back. An old picture with only three faces was sent to the manufacturer, so the emblem on the jackets is missing the face of Roosevelt. The fans bought white and red jackets with the emblem on the back and wore them to all the games.

On top of car Gutzon Borglum, center, Nick Clifford, right, and Red Anderson. Inside of car Howdy Peterson, right, and Merle Peterson. The Keystone team stopped briefly in Rapid City en route to the State Amateur Baseball Tournament in Aberdeen. Borglum, sponsor of the team, accompanied the players as far as Rapid City. The team made the trip to Aberdeen in the station wagon shown in the picture.

Did you know Mr. Borglum?

Q&A   Yes, I knew Mr. Borglum. I rode from Aberdeen to Keystone with him and his driver, Elmer Conklin, after winning the baseball game with Brookings. He was quiet and did not talk much. The two-way roads were gravel in the 1930s, and I remember when we got behind a truck it was really dusty. Mr. Borglum would say to Elmer, "Pass him, pass him," and if the truck driver would not slow down so we could pass, then when we did get a chance to pass, he shook his fist at the truck driver as we went by. Mr. Borglum's car was a Packard.

The next day I rode back to Aberdeen with Duke Peterson and my mother for the game on Sunday afternoon. Duke had two brothers, Merle and Howdy, who played on the Rushmore team.

Baseball jackets. Note the emblem with only three faces.

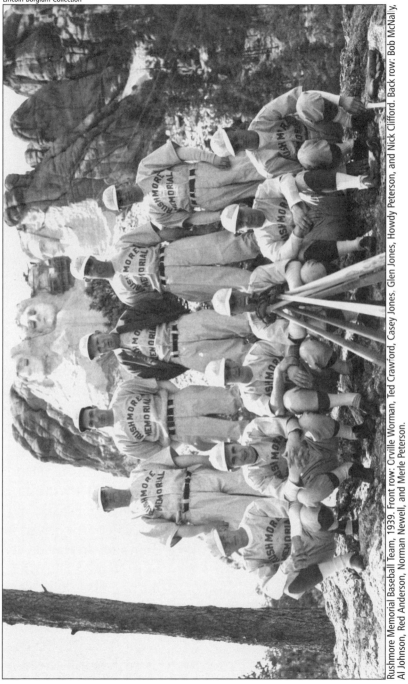

Rushmore Memorial Baseball Team, 1939. Front row: Orville Worman, Ted Crawford, Casey Jones, Glen Jones, Howdy Peterson, and Nick Clifford. Back row: Bob McNally, Al Johnson, Red Anderson, Norman Newell, and Merle Peterson.

Did you come to work [at Mount Rushmore] because of the work or the baseball?

I came for the work. Rushmore was a good place to work. I needed a job and baseball was an extra benefit. I also played baseball with the Junior Legion team in Rapid City.

Where was the ballpark?

The baseball diamond in Keystone was where the National Presidential Wax Museum is currently located. Home plate was backed up to the hillside and the road (to Mount Rushmore) was the outer boundary. If a batter hit the ball across the road it was a home run.

Baseball from Tournament Game
August 31, 1939
Rushmore 2 - Brookings 0

Signed by: Glen Jones, Nick Clifford, Casey Jones, Mickey McGaa, Howard Peterson, Merle Peterson, AO Worman, Lincoln Borglum, Al Johnson, *plus* a few names unable to read, *and* some Brookings players.
Missing names: Ted Crawford & Norman Newell

Did you continue to play baseball after 1940?

We had a team at Rushmore in 1940, but not a very good one because many of the players had left the mountain for steady jobs in California. I played for Tom's Bar in Rapid City in 1941 and 1942. After moving to Custer, SD in 1947 I played on the Custer team for three years. That was the end of my baseball career.

What happened to the uniforms?

I wish I knew what happened to the uniforms. Some of us from Rushmore played on the Tom's Bar team in Rapid City, and all the players wore the Rushmore Memorial uniforms, but the uniforms have not been located since then. I regret not saving my baseball glove.

Surprisingly, the baseball from the tournament game that we won in 1939 has surfaced recently. Ted

Rushmore Nine Trims Brookings In 10-Inning State Meet Thriller

Rapid City Journal, September 1, 1939

Aberdeen, Sept. 1 --(AP)-- Gerry Hertz, big right-hander whose pitching feats form some of the most brilliant chapters in the history of the state amateur baseball tournament, hurled the greatest game of his career yesterday—and lost it.

Young Ted Crawford, a slight left-hander, led an underdog Rushmore team to a 2 to 0 victory over Hertz and his Brookings mates in a stirring 10-inning drama that climaxed yesterday's round of play.

Over 2,000 fans saw the Aberdeen Transfer conquer the Indian team from Little Eagle, 5 to 3, in another great game after Pierre had downed an out-classed young Watertown club, 14 to 2.

Ed Many Deeds, Sr., gallant old warrior who heads the Little Eagle team, stole a large portion of the day's honors by smashing two mighty home runs against Aberdeen, but nothing in the state classic's history surpasses the duel that Hertz and Crawford waged. For nine innings neither gave up a run, Hertz allowing only two men to reach first base, and Crawford reaching sensational heights in the clutches to turn back Brookings' threats.

Both teams played brilliant ball afield and there wasn't an error in the contest, but there's a limit to endurance, and the deadlock broke in the tenth. Hertz walked Catcher McNally with one away in that inning. Then right-fielder Don Clifford smashed a line drive triple into right centerfield to send McNally home with the run that meant victory. Clifford scored the second on a passed ball. Ironically enough, Hertz had just struck out Jones, Rushmore second baseman, to complete a full nine innings of no-hit, no-run pitching before Clifford walked up to the plate.

The score by innings:

Little Eagle	000 000 102	– 3
Aberdeen	300 002 00x	– 5
Watertown	000 100 010	– 2
Pierre	304 312 10x	–14
Rushmore	000 000 000	– 2
Brookings	000 000 000	– 0

Crawford, the winning pitcher, kept the ball for sixty-four years and he gave the ball to me because I was the one who drove in the winning runs in the tenth inning. Lincoln Borglum and most of the players signed the ball. Along with the jackets and other baseball memorabilia, the ball is on display in the Lincoln Borglum Visitor Center at Mount Rushmore.

Griff's
GRAFFS
By Raymond S. Griffiths
JOURNAL SPORTS EDITOR

ONE OF THE STATE'S BEST KNOWN UMPIRES, Ben "Mac" McKeague of Aberdeen, is now Aviation mechanic instructor at The NYA center in Rapid City...

... McKeague is not only a personified rule book, but he recalls every outstanding incident and just how it happened in every game he has seen or umpired.

"The greatest game I ever worked was the Rushmore-Brookings battle in 1939," he recalls, and undoubtedly there are few to compare with it in state amateur annals.

The game was a pitcher's duel between young Ted Crawford, slight left-hander for Rushmore, and Gerry Hertz, ace Brookings moundsman. Rushmore was the underdog and for nine innings Hertz failed to give up a hit. Neither team made a single error in the entire game. Crawford came through in the clutches and beat down Brookings' threats while his mates gave him airtight support.

In the 10th inning Bob McNally, Rushmore catcher, walked. Donald "Nick" Clifford then tripled and scored McNally. Clifford came in on a wild pitch, the only bobble of the day and the game ended 2 to 0.

"It was the tensest game I ever worked, and also the quietest with every player intent on his work," McKeague said. "In a lopsided game an umpire is inclined to loaf, but when things are nip-and-tuck a man is on his toes every second and can't afford to miss anything."

The slender "umps" is one of the state's most ardent baseball fans and followers of every phase of the sport.

Excerpted from the *Rapid City Journal* (1940s).

Dear Mrs. Borglum - we are winning! The first game, on Monday, we defeated Woonsocket 5 to 1 . . . then had to wait over til yesterday (Thursday) for our really hard game with Brookings, who had been pretty generally picked as state champion. Mr B and Elmer came down to see it, and of course all "the boys" were delighted to have Mr B here. And what a game! nine innings with no scoring, no errors – gosh, how excited we all were! Finally in the first half of the tenth inning McNally was walked, then little Nickie Clifford came thru with a three base hit, pushing McNally in for a score – and Nickie sneaked in too – anyway, we won - 2 to 0 – and the boys are still celebrating! Mr B invited all of them and their wives, and all of the Brookings team and their wives to a dinner party – which they all loved – really was a fine gesture. Mr B and Elmer, and Clifford, went back to Rushmore this morning; the rest of us waiting for our next game on Sunday, which should be an easy one – then the finals on Monday . . . which we have a swell chance for if only we can manage to keep the team together – there's so much bickering among them, as usual! Frightfully hot here, and even the little showers we've had make it hotter – like a steam bath! We go out to see the other teams play all afternoon, and bowl at night, and talk endlessly about baseball!! There was a picture of Lincoln in the paper the other day, in which he looks so like his father – I'll try to find it and enclose it – and another one this morning – everyone here in Aberdeen was so pleased that Mr B came and made a great deal over him – and how he enjoyed the game! Gosh, here I am back at baseball again! I reckon I'd better close anyway, Lincoln and I are going shopping for a stone crock in which to make peach brandy – we've still got that on our minds despite all this baseball. We'll be expecting you home very soon now – please don't disappoint us! Lincoln joins me in sending lots of love to you -

Sept 1'39

Louella

The above letter dated September 1, 1939, was written by Louella Jones Borglum to her mother-in-law, Mrs. Gutzon Borglum. Lincoln and Louella Borglum were attending the State Amateur Baseball Tournament in Aberdeen. The letter is reprinted as typed by Louella.

At age 70, Nick returned to the top of the mountain for the first time in fifty-one years.

CHAPTER 10

Personal Experiences and Reflections

Was it prestigious working on Mount Rushmore?

No, not really. Many people thought Mr. Borglum was crazy to start a project like this. Today it has become very special to me because not many men have a chance to help carve a mountain.

How does it feel to have this kind of excitement in your life?

At the time I never thought anything about it. Working on Mount Rushmore was a fairly good job, and I was happy to have a job that paid well. Nowadays as I look back, I feel very honored to have worked on a great piece of history such as Mount Rushmore.

Was it hard?

Yes. It was dusty, dirty, noisy and just plain hard work. When you are young you can do hard work. Eventually I got "toughened in" and the hard work did not bother me much. The hardest part was running a jackhammer. Cranking the men up and down in the winch house was an easier job.

Was this work harder than in the mines?

I do not think so; the two jobs were very different. Working in the mines required a lot of lifting, whereas my job on the mountain required running a jackhammer or another air tool most of the time. There was much more dust created at the mountain.

Are you afraid of heights?

When a person is young, at least in my case, I was not afraid of much. Today you could not pay me enough to go over the side of the mountain in a harness!

In 1991 I walked to the top of the mountain for the first time in fifty-one years. Several television networks followed President George Bush to Mount Rushmore when he came for the 50th Anniversary. The network and newspaper reporters interviewed many of the former workers at that time. I was interviewed in front of Lincoln's chin not far from the area where I drilled in 1940 (see photo on page 54).

" While shaking hands with a little three-year-old boy Nick said, "Come back to Mount Rushmore when you get big." "I'm already big!" he shouted. **"**

Was there a road to Rushmore from Keystone?

The first road was not much more than a horse trail, although some cars made it up the trail. President Calvin Coolidge rode up on horseback when he came for the first dedication commemorating the start of construction on August 10, 1927. The highway department continued to improve the road so today it is a very good highway following much the same route as in 1927.

What was a day like?

Most of the men lived in Keystone, but everyone did not drive his own car to work. We rode together and took turns driving from week to week. Usually the men who lived in the same neighborhood rode together. It took about fifteen minutes to drive up to the mountain.

We had to be on the mountain ready for work when the whistle blew at 7:30 a.m. In earlier years when the men walked up the wooden stairs, they had to judge for themselves how long it would take. When I was working we rode up in the bucket, which made more than one trip, so we had to allow for that.

Every day the work was much the same. As a driller I drilled holes eight hours a day, six days a week. It was hard work! Whatever the weather, we just went to work and made the best of it.

Did you drive your 1926 Chevrolet Touring Car to work?

In 1938 and 1939 I drove to work and another man rode with me until I cracked the block on it. I paid $25 for the car and wish I still had it.

How did you crack the block on your car?

In those days we did not have anti-freeze, so at night we had to drain the water from the radiator and fill it up again in the morning. One morning the man riding with me did not get the petcock closed after filling the radiator; as a result we were out of water halfway to the mountain. We stopped at a spring along the way and put cold water in the hot radiator, which cracked the block, of course.

How did you stand the heat day after day?

I do not recall the heat being so bad, although I am sure it was. The dust was worse than the heat. Eventually a person adjusted to the elements, and they did not bother so much. I was lucky to have a job.

How did you dress to stay warm when it was cold?

I never wore long underwear, although I am sure some men wore it. On a cold day we wore bib overalls, heavy socks, jackets, gloves and caps with ear covers. The cold was not so bad because nobody worked during the winter months, except in 1938, and that year I was working down below the faces.

What did a worker take in his lunch box for lunch?

Usually lunch was one or two sandwiches made with white bread - my favorite was a meat loaf sandwich. In those days sandwiches often were made with leftovers from dinner the night before. We would have cake, cookies, and maybe an apple. Many men had a thermos of coffee, but I do not remember drinking coffee. We did not have potato chips, soft drinks, and a variety of snack foods then.

What is your best memory? Then and now?

Now my best memory is having the opportunity to work on the mountain carving. Knowing Mr. Borglum, Lincoln Borglum, and many of the men who helped carve the mountain means a lot to me today, especially when I see people coming from all over the world to view the monument. These men and their stories are all gone now.

The most memorable time then was when we had our good baseball team and the workmen would guess the outcome of the games coming up that weekend.

What was the worst part and the scariest part of the job?

The dust was the worst part of the job. It would get into your eyes, ears, hair, nose, and worst of all, your throat. It was a dirty job and hard work.

To me there was no particular scary part. As I look back, maybe riding up in the bucket each morning was the scariest part.

Did you have job security working at Mount Rushmore?

No. There was no job security, but if you were a good worker and did your job, then you were likely to stay on the job. When the money was spent the workers never knew whether the federal government would make another appropriation for work to continue.

What did you do when the mountain shut down?

We tried to save enough money from our summer wages to carry us through the winter. When there was other work around Keystone we would get another job, then most of us would return to the mountain in the spring. It was a bigger hardship on the married men with families to support.

Did they treat you very well?

Personally, I had no complaints. Lincoln Borglum was always on the mountain, so if anyone had any problems we could go to him. Lincoln was such a great guy and he always went out of his way to help a man. All the workmen had nothing but good things to say about Lincoln.

> **An emotional lady told Nick after talking with him about Mount Rushmore, "I think I'm in love with you."**
>
> **"Well, I love you for coming to see Mount Rushmore!" Nick responded.**

Was this the focal point of your life?

As I look back, maybe it was. I think I have had my share of good things in life.

Did you feel like an artist when you were working on something the whole world would come to see?

No. I did not feel like an artist, nor do I feel like one today. Mr. Borglum was the artist, and a very good one. Some of the men that were trained by the artist as finish carvers worked many years and got very good at their jobs. Perhaps they could be called artists.

How old were you when you got this job?

I was seventeen when I got the job and I worked three years at Mount Rushmore. Some of the workmen were in their forties and fifties.

Where did you live?

I lived with my mother in the small town of Keystone, three miles from the mountain.

When construction started in 1927 I was only six years old, so I grew up with the mountain. I delivered the *Rapid City Journal* to many of the men who worked at Mount Rushmore and knew most of them.

Was your mother worried about you?

I do not think so; at least she never said anything to me about it. I know she was happy I had a job!

How did you get the nickname "Nick" from Donald?

There were five children in my family and we all had nicknames. No one told me how I ended up with Nick, but it stayed with me all my life.

More than a hundred of the 395 names on the Workers Recognition Plaque have nicknames, which indicates that many people were known by a nickname in those days.

Nick's mother, Margaret Clifford, left, and Mollie Sagdalen on top of Mount Rushmore in the 1920s.

What was one of the practical jokes played on you?

Because I was the youngest worker I received my share of practical jokes, all in fun, of course. One morning five of us were at the hoist house waiting to go up in the bucket when the other four men grabbed me and nailed my shoes to the platform. Mr. Borglum generally did not come to the mountain before 7 a.m., but that particular day he was early. As he walked past me, I stood nailed to the platform with my arms folded looking up at the mountain pretending to be a tourist. Fortunately for me, he walked right by me.

Usually I could think of some way to retaliate! That day I waited until after work. Our lunch boxes were sent down in the bucket after lunch and Ed Hayes, who worked in the hoist house, always lined them up on the platform to be picked up after work. I made sure I was down before the men who had nailed me to the platform so I could nail their lunch boxes to the platform. They ended up with some bent lunch boxes and I ended up with holes in the soles of my shoes.

> " An elderly woman, traveling with her niece, felt rushed by the younger woman. Nick said to her, "Rush, rush, huh!" She agreed. "That's why it's called Rushmore!" she added. "

Q Can you think of any other jokes played on you?

A One day after work I found my car on top of the sand pile by the Sculptor's Studio. With a lot of shoveling I managed to get it down so I could drive home.

The workers used to play practical jokes on the visitors too. Quite often we glued a coin to the platform, then stood back to watch someone try to pick it up. A visitor told me that joke actually happened to him and his parents when they came to Mount Rushmore in 1939. He said it was one of the few things that he remembered from that trip.

Did mountain goats live around here in the 1930s?

We never saw any mountain goats when we were carving the mountain, but now they live in this area. Occasionally a goat is spotted walking up the muck pile below the faces.

Was it sad when the project ended?

It was sad when Mr. Borglum died, ending all the struggles and frustrations that went on over the years. Knowing the sculpture probably never would be completed and knowing we were engaging in another war also made it a sad time for us.

Clifford family photo (1942)

Nick Clifford (right) and Ed Hayes working at the Etta Mine.

63

Mt. Rushmore Memorial 25th Anniversary – August 11, 1952 – Custer State Park
Top Row: R.G. Kingsbury, Orville Worman, Charles Hallsted, Alton Leach, Robert Himebaugh, Don Morrison, Ed Hallsted, Gus Schramm, Edwald Hayes, Dick Huntimer. *Center Row:* Mrs. Gale Wilcox, Mrs. O.H. Wilcox, Mrs. O.H. Wilcox, Mrs. Otto Anderson, Jack Zasadil, John Lintz, Donald "Nick" Clifford, Basil Canfield, Ernest Raga, Glenn Bradford, Lloyd Virtue, Miles Gardner, Raleigh Crane. *Front Row:* Rev. C.H. Loocke, G.R. Jurisch, Merle Peterson, Otto Anderson, Joe Bruner, Alvin Bradford, John Boland, Howard Peterson, Gale Wilcox, Owen Mann.

What did you do after you left the mountain?

In 1941 several of the workers assumed federal funding would end. Some of us went back to work in the mines in Keystone. Others went to California where good jobs were plentiful and year around.

I went to work in the Etta Mine in Keystone. The following year I got married and went into the military for four years. I served two years in the European Theater in the Air Force Signal Corps. In May 1946, I received an honorable discharge.

Do you have any children?

I have two daughters and one son, two granddaughters and one grandson, three great-granddaughters, and one great-grandson.

How did you spend the rest of your life?

Following my discharge I worked in the mines again for a short while. Then I moved to Igloo, SD where my brother, Francis, taught me the dry cleaning business. I owned and operated a dry cleaning shop in Custer, SD for the next ten years. From 1957 through 1967 I operated Sylvan Lake Resort in Custer State Park, SD. When my lease expired I moved to Houston, TX so I could attend baseball games in the newly built Astrodome.

Carolyn [Moen] and I were married in 1974 in Houston. We soon moved back to Keystone and opened the Dip-A-Lot Ice Cream and Sandwich Shop, which we operated for four years. After that I was ready to retire!

" With tears in his eyes, a gentleman told Nick, "I will never look at the mountain with quite the same feeling again now that I have met someone who was there. Thank you for sharing your story." "

Conclusion

Life Makes a Full Circle

Nick is one of the rare individuals whose experiences in life have come full circle. In 1997 Nick and his wife, Carolyn, purchased the old house in Keystone where Nick's family lived and struggled. Built in 1895 and in disrepair, Nick and Carolyn restored the structure and filled the small house with family heirlooms. Nick's former bedroom measures six feet by eight feet.

Nick and Carolyn are happy they live close to Mount Rushmore so they can visit often. They enjoy telling about Nick's first-hand experiences and answering many questions. Nick said, "I plan to stay close to Mount Rushmore because it is an important part of my life now." Pausing, he added, "It makes me proud to be an American to have worked on something like this."

Nick Clifford grew up in the house on the right with his brothers and sisters, Charles, Francis, Margaret and Jeannette. Their mother, Margaret Stangle Clifford, paid $147 for the house at a 1933 tax sale. On the left is the historic Keystone School, built in 1899. The 4th Cavalry from Fort Meade, SD on bivouac at Keystone, is in the foreground.

Photo courtesy of the Halley family collection

Clifford family photo (1999)

Nick and Carolyn Clifford purchased Nick's boyhood home at auction in 1997. The above photo, taken after they restored the house, is located on the corner of Mitchell and Second Streets in Keystone, SD. Below: Carolyn and Nick in the parlor of their restored house.

Clifford family photo (1999)

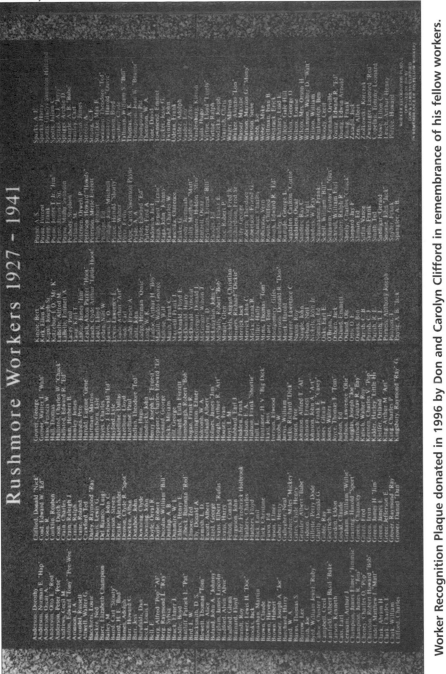

Worker Recognition Plaque donated in 1996 by Don and Carolyn Clifford in remembrance of his fellow workers.